Brain BENDERS

AMAZING FACTS

ARCTURUS

ARCTURUS

This edition published in 2017 by Arcturus Publishing Limited
26/27 Bickels Yard, 151–153 Bermondsey Street,
London SE1 3HA

ISBN: 978-1-78828-065-5
CH005927NT
Supplier 10, Date 0817, Print run 6327

Illustrations by Andy Peters

Printed in the UK

CONTENTS

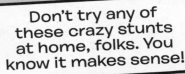

Don't try any of these crazy stunts at home, folks. You know it makes sense!

Totally Crazy!

Keep your eyes peeled for these facts. They're so off the wall, they deserve a special mention!

CHAPTER 1
Animal Antics

The animal world is filled with all manner of weird and wonderful creatures. Many find a place in our home and end up soiling the carpet! But animals are capable of so much more than that. Read on, and you'll find yourself wondering whether we humans really are the smartest critters on the planet.

Ninja Chimp

If he were still alive, Charlie the Chimp could show Jackie Chan a thing or two. Charlie, a chimpanzee, was awarded a black belt for his amazing display of karate skills in 1987. After becoming world famous, he enjoyed the high life. As well as touring the United States and showing off his technique, he appeared on television shows and in movies. He died in 2013.

Time to Chill

In between bouts of sparring, Charlie liked to relax by playing in his pool, reading magazines, and feasting on tasty snacks.

Stats 'n' Facts

Name: Charlie the Chimp
Weight: 90 kg/198 lb
Owner: Carmen Presti
Home: Niagara Falls, New York, USA
Fave food: Pizza, chicken wings
Fact: Charlie was heavier than martial arts king Bruce Lee.

Guess What?

Charlie had an arch rival in the shape of a monkey from Japan who could chop panels of wood in two with his bare hands!

Fashion Victims

While most countries like to watch their guinea pigs play in cages, the people of Peru prefer to dress them up.

Every year, in Huacho, Peru, the Festival of the Guinea Pig takes place. People flock to see these cute, furry creatures dressed up as miners, peasants, kings, and queens. Then they judge which one is best dressed.

Piggy Olympics

In 2006, 12 little piggies went to Moscow, Russia, to compete in the third annual Pig Olympics.

Attracting entrants from seven different countries, including South Africa and Ukraine, the special Olympics were made up of three events:

★ A running race featuring obstacles and jumps

★ A swimming event with pigs paddling across a pool

★ A game where a ball covered in fish oil (yuk!) was pushed around until a pig scored a goal.

Mighty Mouse House

It may not be a luxury penthouse, but the humble tennis ball is keeping the harvest mouse alive.

Harvest mice were rapidly becoming Great Britain's No. 1 snack for animal predators, so they started building nests in safer places above ground. Then wildlife experts stepped in and gave them a plump tennis ball with a hole in it, to sleep in instead!

Nest Building

The tennis ball is attached to a pole above the ground. A hole is cut, and a seed is placed inside. The mouse climbs in to get the seed, then snoozes!

Guess What?

The balls used to shelter the harvest mice come from Wimbledon, UK, the home of one of the world's greatest tennis tournaments.

Stats 'n' Facts

Name: Harvest mouse
Latin name: *Micromys minutus*
Home: Europe and Asia
Looks: Brown and furry
Fact: Harvest mice are tiny, about the size of a coin.

7

Surf's Up, Ratty

Totally Crazy!

They're best known for spreading the bubonic plague, but did you know some rats are also surfboarding stars? Yes, really!

Fin and Tofu were two one-year-old rats who dazzled onlookers at the beach with their surfboarding tricks. They rode 1.2 m/4 ft waves and surfed through "tubes" (tunnels of water) for up to 20 minutes at a time. Thanks to their owner's training, these young rats fell off their boards less than most human surfers!

"Running on a wheel isn't enough for Fin and Tofu; they like a more extreme rush!"
Owner, Boomer Hodel

Guess What?

The surfing rodents were fed on a high-protein, low-carbohydrate diet to help keep them in tip-top shape for their antics on the waves.

Stats 'n' Facts

Names: Fin and Tofu
Home: Oahu, Hawaii, USA
Owner: Boomer Hodel
Lifestyle: Beach bums
Fact: The rats owned their own special surfboards.

8

Cat-astrophically Fat

Kitty lovers, think again. Put that tuna away! It's time to meet some of the world's fattest cats.

★ Katy was a noisy Siamese cat that lived in the Ural Mountains, Russia. Siamese cats are normally sleek and slender but not Katy. In 2003, she weighed in at a whopping 22.5 kg/50 lb, about the size of a six-year-old boy.

★ Samson, a beautiful Maine coon cat, lives with owner Jonathan Zurbel and is a fab 'n' furry 1.2 m/4 ft long and 13 kg/28 lb. He has been called the toast of New York City.

★ Perhaps the most infamous fat cat was Tiddles, a stray adopted by a worker at Paddington Station, London, UK. Tiddles became a star and received fan mail from his fans.

Guess What?

There are no longer any official records kept for fat cats. This is to stop encouraging people from overfeeding their pets.

Gobble It Up

Katy's owner claimed that her cat didn't eat that much food. But she also claimed that Katy could wolf down a hot dog in under a minute!

9

Salty Seafarer

Rats adore the water, but none more so than one incredible rodent found off the coast of New Zealand.

In 2005, scientists radio-tagged a Norway rat for a study. However, it made a break for freedom and swam an amazing 400 m/1,312 ft in the sea before being recaptured. Some people think that the intrepid swimmer may have set a new world record for a rat swimming in open water.

Wheelie Lucky

Totally Crazy!

You usually expect to see broken-down cars on roads with multiple lanes, but how about ... a hamster?

British drivers were amazed one day in 2006, when they spotted a hamster running along inside a plastic exercise ball on a major road. Roly, as he was nicknamed, was rescued by animal welfare workers. He was not prosecuted for driving without a permit!

Doggy Masterpieces

The very idea might have had Van Gogh cutting his ear off in despair, but some dogs can actually paint.

The Shore Service Dogs in the UK are trained to help disabled people, but they like doing a little artistic creation on the side. Their owner, Mary Stadelbacher, says the dogs paint bright, abstract pictures. Their work fetches up to £1,000/$1,280 per piece.

Paw Prints

Each dog-painted picture is signed with a black paw print by the canine artist responsible. So look closely the next time you see some art on a wall!

Guess What?

Stadelbacher doesn't claim that her dogs are the first to put paw to print, but she does believe they are the first to use an actual brush.

"Go paint, Sammy!" calls Mary Stadelbacher to her dogs during demonstrations.

Smooching Pooches

If 356 dogs turn up to get married, it can't really be wrong!

In 2007, Littleton, Colorado, USA, a group of dog owners oversaw an arranged marriage for their canine pets. On the big day, the loved-up pooches swapped their collars for full wedding attire and took their "bow-wow vows."

If a pet wedding like this takes your fancy, you can hire a wedding planner. They will plan:

★ The perfect outfits: tuxedo, dress, and veil
★ A doggy marriage certificate
★ Wedding cake and canine treats.

We're not making this up!

"It was time to make it legal. Dezi is totally in love with Lucy."
Mother of Lucy the dog, one of the brides-to-be

Guess What?

The dog wedding in Littleton smashed the previous record held by the Netherlands. At the Dutch ceremony, only 54 loved-up pooches tied the knot.

Firefighters to the Rescue

What do you do if your hamster gets its head stuck between the bars of its cage?

It's obvious, of course. You call in the firefighters. That's exactly what the owner of a cute little hamster from Cheshire, UK, did when its head got wedged between the narrow metal bars of its cage. Luckily, in no time at all, the firefighters freed the furry critter, and it lived to tell the tale.

Nuclear Kitty

Is it possible for a cat to grow grotesquely fat after being exposed to nuclear radiation?

Roger Degange shot to fame in 2001 when he claimed that his cat, Snowball, became obese because she had been wandering around a deserted nuclear facility. Sounds ridiculous? Well, it is! The cruel prankster had just overfed her.

Pygmy Up, Please

The world's officially smallest monkey was a baby pygmy marmoset.

The tiny primate was a mere 35 cm/13.7 in tall when fully grown and weighed 100 g/ 3.5 oz. But beware, this animal wasn't as cute a pet as it sounds. Expect a monkey to bite, scratch, and cause damage all around the house!

Tall Tails

In 2008, Summer Breeze, the American Paint Horse, had a record-breaking tail, more than 3.81 m/12.5 ft long, about the length of a car.

Owner Crystal Socha kept Summer's tail braided and covered in a tube sock when not showing her off. She combed and shampooed the tail every two months. It took three hours at a time to complete this Herculean task because each hair is as fine as a fishing line.

Frog of Many Talents

Performing frogs are something of a rarity, unless you're Nong Oui from Thailand.

Able to sit on a toy motorcycle and more than happy to be handled, Nong Oui caused quite a splash when she was shown to reporters. But it was her talent for predicting lottery numbers that made her an even bigger froggy hit!

Grounded

Sadly, Nong Oui's owner had to ground her when the frog's run of luck ended, and she stopped predicting the winning lottery numbers.

Stats 'n' Facts

Name: Nong Oui
Type: Black-spotted frog
Home: Thailand
Hobbies: Riding toy vehicles
Fact: As well as Harley Davidson's, Nong Oui liked to ride garbage trucks.

Guess What?

Locals examined the patterns on Nong Oui's skin to find their lottery numbers. The amazing clairvoyant frog came up trumps 10 times in a row.

15

Squirrels on the Water

To older people, Twiggy is the name of a model who wore miniskirts. To animal lovers, she's a waterskiing squirrel.

Twiggy is a squirrel from Florida, USA, who has been trained to waterski by the Best family since the late 1970s using a remote-controlled boat. She's a huge hit with the American public and has appeared on many TV shows. She's even starred in big Hollywood movies, including *Dodgeball* and *Anchorman*.

"Twiggy is really quite happy with her life. She has her own room at home with trees to climb."

Lou Ann Best, dismissing complaints from animal rights campaigners

Murky Secret

Twiggy, who has been waterskiing for nearly 40 years, is actually a series of squirrels that go by the same name. Squirrels only live for about six years.

Get a Pet-icure

Totally Crazy!

If you want a set of perfect feet, then you'll need 5,000 flesh-eating fish to do the job.

When razors were banned for use in pedicures in the state of Virginia, USA, salon owner Yvonne Le scoured the Internet to find an alternative. She hit the jackpot when she discovered the garra rufa fish: It loves nibbling away at dead skin! Customers have described the sensation as being like hundreds of delicate kisses.

My Teeny Tiny Pony

Need the perfect pet to walk in the park? Try the world's smallest horse, Thumbelina from Missouri, USA.

Thumbelina comes from a genuine miniature horse breed, but she's also a dwarf, which makes her extra-small and extra-special. She's only about 44 cm/17 in tall. Thumbelina is nicknamed "Mini Mini" by her owners. They say she likes nothing better than bossing the bigger horses around!

You Calling Me Ugly?

Every year in Petaluma, California, USA, the world's ugliest dog competition takes place.

Dog owners from across the country travel to the contest to show off their pets' challenging looks. The 2008 winner was Gus, from Florida. Poor old Gus had just one eye after a fight with a tomcat and only three legs. However, his owner loved him just the same!

Hamster Escapes a Hammering

Cats are supposed to have nine lives, but daring Mike the hamster from North Wales, UK, runs an extremely close second.

In 2006, Mike had an incredible escape from a shredder and three different kinds of crushing machine in an industrial waste unit. He was spun, shaken, and nearly squashed to death before popping out at the other end unharmed after a four-minute destruction process. That's one lucky hamster!

Look Up That Tree!

Totally Crazy!

Everyone knows that sure-footed goats are great at climbing mountains, but a few also like to climb trees!

In southwest Morocco, the amazing local goats scale seriously high branches to feed on the delicious berries found in argan trees. But that's not their only skill. They also help the local women to make argan oil from the berries, which is used for cooking and beauty treatments.

Oil Recipe

Once the goats have eaten their fill, they poo out the kernels from the berry seed. Local women pick them up and grind them to make the argan oil.

Stats 'n' Facts

Local name: "Ha-ha" goat
Latin name: *Capra hircus*
Home: Morocco
Looks: Black, white, brown
Fact: Some goats have been spotted balancing up to 9 m/ 30 ft high in the branches.

Guess What?

Not all Argan oil is made from goat droppings. Modern machinery can make the oil directly from the berries. It's just not quite the same!

CHAPTER 2
Ridiculous Objects

Useless, oversized, or bizarrely shaped: You can guarantee you'll find an everyday object that's been "ridiculized." For years, madcap inventors have been busy in their sheds or garages, dedicating their lives to developing alternatives to everyday items and making the world laugh.

Moving Along

Sometimes a boring old car isn't enough, especially when you can have one in the shape of a cricket bat!

India's Sudhakar Yadav is a man with a mission. He's built over 200 motorized vehicles in the shape of everything from footballs to hamburgers. All of them, including his nutty motorized cricket bat car, work. Check out more of his creations below:

★ A two-seater Valentine's car adorned with hearts and roses for loved-up couples who want to take a ride

★ A world-record-breaking tricycle that is a staggering 12.5 m/41 ft tall and took three years to build!

Stats 'n' Facts

Name: Cricket bat car
Top speed: 60 kmh/40 mph
Time to build: Six months
Cost: Approx £1,000/$1,280
Fact: The cricket bat car was built to celebrate India in the 2007 Cricket World Cup.

Guess What?

You can see all of Sudhakar's vehicles in his museum in Hyderbad, India. The place is extremely popular, attracting up to 1,000 visitors a day.

Rotating Fork

If you like spaghetti but have a hard time twirling it around your fork, then this is the invention for you.

Invented by Mr. Kenji Kawakami (see page 24), the rotating spaghetti fork is ideal for lazy foodies everywhere. However, there is one major problem. Imagine the spaghetti wrapping automatically around the fork ... great. Now imagine the pasta sauce flying everywhere ... not so great!

Giant Board Game

A board game can get boring ... but not when it's a giant version of Monopoly with houses and hotels 1,700 times larger than their original size!

To play the mammoth board game, head to Monopoly in the Park, in San Jose, California, USA. The 86 sq m/926 sq ft board is the largest outdoor version of the game in the world. Expect to wear huge token-shaped hats and a prison outfit if you get sent to jail.

A Truckload of Art

Is it a work of art or just plain ridiculous? Make your own mind up about the crazy Big Rig Jig sculpture.

Created in 2007 by US artist Mike Ross for the Burning Man Festival, the sculpture featured two full-sized 18-wheeler tanker trucks, towering four floors high. Behind the craziness, there was a serious message about how the oil industry has a powerful hold over our global society. Make of it what you like!

"... it should give you a sense of danger and fear, and that something is wrong."
Artist Mike Ross talking about his towering tanker sculpture

Guess What?

Artist Ross created a smaller plastic model before beginning the full-sized piece, so he could be sure his mega sculpture would work.

Stats 'n' Facts

Name: Big Rig Jig
What: Giant sculpture
Where: Nevada, USA
Why: For The Burning Man experimental art festival
Fact: Every year, a giant wooden effigy is burned at the festival.

The Art of Chindogu

Totally Crazy!

When is an invention useless but also useful? Welcome to the Japanese art of Chindogu!

Mr. Kenji Kawakami is the creator of Chindogu, which loosely translated means "unusual tool." He has invented hundreds of absurd items that have become strangely popular. Check these out:

★ An outdoor toilet seat with artificial grass to keep your bottom warm
★ A two-way sandal with toes at both ends, so you can wear it both ways
★ An alarm clock with sharp pins on the off button that prick you when you try to turn it off.

> "People need to laugh for no reason ... The concept is: You have it, I have it, everybody has this wackiness."
>
> Kenji Kawakami explains why he continues with Chindogu

Guess What?

There is method behind the inventor's madness. He believes that his ideas could make us question our views on consumerism.

Tour de Farce

Next time you see the Tour de France on TV, keep your eyes peeled for a red devil towing a giant bicycle.

German-born Dieter "Didi" Senft can regularly be found following the famous Tour de France cycling competition dressed up as the devil. El Diablo, as he is known, has been cheering on the riders for years. He paints a devil's pitchfork on the road several hours beforehand to announce his arrival.

Bathroom Car

A toilet-shaped car is the way to go if you want to make a splash! At least, if you are K. Sudhakar of Hyderabad, India, that is.

Featuring a 50 cc engine and boasting a top speed of 40 kmh/25 mph, Sudhakar's crazy car definitely gets noticed. The driver sits in the bowl with the lid up and zooms along. Thankfully, the toilet shape is an arresting design feature only: You aren't actually supposed to use it as a moving bathroom!

Hay Fever Hat

It's not attractive, and you'll get funny looks in the street, but your nose will thank you for wearing this hat.

Japanese inventor Kenji Kawakami (see page 24) has created a bizarre hat for hay fever sufferers or indeed anyone who has the sniffles. Just reach up, unroll your toilet tissue, and blow your nose. You'll never be caught with dangling snot again!

Topsy-Turvy Houses

There are several upside-down houses around the world with their roofs stuck in the ground, but only a few have their interiors upside down, too.

Take a trip to the German island of Usedom, and you'll discover a house that you enter through the attic. Inside, chairs, tables, and carpets are upside down. Even the bathrooms are topsy-turvy. The house is part of a project called "The World on Its Head." Other brain-straining exhibits are planned.

Crazy Bikes

When he's not dressed up as the devil (see page 25), German "Didi" Senft indulges his other passion: building bizarre bicycles.

Didi has built over 120 bonkers bicycles and has won multiple world records. One of his wacky inventions is the world's biggest mobile guitar.

To pedal it, Didi lies flat on his back beneath a stonking half ton of metal.

His other crazy creations include a World Cup tricycle featuring 100 soccer balls incorporated into its design.

Stats 'n' Facts

Name: Mobile guitar
Length: 40 m/131 ft
Height: 4.2 m/13.8 ft
Fact: More than 300 m/ 980 ft of metal piping was used to build the mobile guitar.

Guess What?

Although Didi has ridden his giant guitar bike around a field, he's not allowed to take it on a public road due to its incredible length.

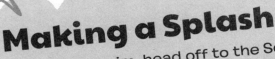

Making a Splash

If you feel like a swim, head off to the South American beach resort of San Alfonso del Mar. But make sure you pack some floats in your suitcase!

The swimming pool at this resort is the largest by area in the world. It took five years to build and measures an area of 8 ha (19.77 acres). To cover one single length, you're in for a 1 km/0.5 mile doggy paddle. But don't worry: If you can't face the distance, you can always jump in a kayak to get across.

Shouting Vase

Totally Crazy!

Feeling angry? Want to vent some frustration? Then try the shouting vase.

Aware that screaming loudly to relieve tension might scare everyone, Kenji Kawakami (see page 24) has thoughtfully invented the shouting vase. Simply put it to your lips, and shout into the opening at the top. The vase muffles the outcry into a whisper, thanks to its soundproofed interior. Genius!

Teeny, Tiny Hard Drive

Computer hard drives are shrinking, but Toshiba has one that is small enough to sit on your finger!

Back in 2004, electronics giant Toshiba unveiled the world's smallest hard drive. It weighed a scanty 2 g/0.004 lb. In 2007, the company boosted the memory from 4 to 8 GB. The hard drive has already been put to good use in a mobile (cell) phone released in Japan.

Board Game Madness

Think that a game of Monopoly can be a drag sometimes? Well, how about playing for 70 straight days, the world record for the longest game of Monopoly ever?

Other crazy board game world records include:

★ Playing them in the bathtub for 99 hours
★ Playing them in a tree house for 286 hours
★ Playing them upside down 36 hours.

Really Weird

The next time you're in Michigan, USA, keep your eyes peeled for Kerry McLean sitting inside a giant rubber wheel ... a monowheel ... motoring along!

Although first proposed in the nineteenth century as a serious means of getting around, today, the monowheel is a cult object. McLean has created a top-of-the-range vehicle, known as the Rocket Roadster, which reaches a staggering speed of 86 kmh/56 mph.

"It's not easy to ride ... It's like riding a wheelie the whole time."

Mark Cernicky, another monowheel expert from *Cycleworld* magazine

Rocket Record

McLean has spent years riding monowheels. With his Rocket Roadster, he held the world land speed record for powered single wheelers for 15 years.

Guess What?

If you want to indulge a passion for riding monowheels, you can. McLean's vehicles are fully road legal and available to buy.

Living in a Toilet

When house prices go down the pan, a toilet-shaped house is the best you can ask for.

Made from steel, glass, and white concrete, the toilet house has two bedrooms, two guest rooms, and ... yes, you've guessed it ... four deluxe bathrooms. Some of the toilets even have motion sensors to lift the lid automatically when they detect your behind.

"The toilet house has become a new cultural icon in the toilet culture movement."
Statement from the World Toilet Association

Rent It

You can rent the toilet house for US $50,000 a day. The money isn't wasted; it's used to aid developing countries.

Stats 'n' Facts

What: Toilet-shaped house
Name: Haewoojae
Where: South Korea
Floor space: 419 sq m/ 4,510 sq ft
Fact: This architectural marvel was built in 2007 for the World Toilet Association.

Guess What?

The toilet house was built by Sim Jae Duck. He is known as Mr. Toilet because of his work trying to turn public facilities into pleasant places.

16,000 for Dinner

In 1998, in Lisbon, Portugal, a huge table was set across the Vasco da Gama bridge for 16,000 hungry diners.

Stretching for 5 km/3 miles and spanning one-third of the length of the bridge, it became the longest dining table ever laid. Guests enjoyed a traditional Portuguese dish, the famous Feijoada stew ... all 10 tons of it.

Pass Me the Butterstick

Totally Crazy!

Fed up of using a knife to butter your toast? Well, try the no-fuss butterstick instead.

Glue meets butter in this silly but smart idea that saves time washing dishes.

Dispensed in a glue applicator-style stick, you just rub the butter directly on your toast, then replace the lid. It's the ultimate in laziness.

The inventor? Of course, it's the irrepressible Mr. Kenji Kawakami, the master of Chindogu (see page 24).

Nano Book

You might get serious eye strain with a book called *The World's Smallest Book*.

The size of a match head and tiny enough to sit on the end of your finger, *The World's Smallest Book* was introduced to the world in 2002 by a German publishing company. To avoid losing it during transit, the leather-bound mini title was delivered in a mahogany box.

"It was printed in the usual way, but all the machinery and tools had to be created in miniature first."

Publisher, Alexander Nedo

Zooming In

To read the contents of the teeny book, the publisher has thoughtfully included a magnifying glass as part of the whole package.

Stats 'n' Facts

What: *The World's Smallest Book*
Size: 2.4 x 2.9 mm/0.09 x 0.11 in
Number of pages: 26
Cost: US $1,000
Fact: There is no plot to this bonsai book. Each page contains a single letter of the alphabet.

Guess What?

A smaller book, *Teeny Ted from Turnip Town*, is a limited edition children's book. It is so tiny, you need a microscope to see it!

Carting It

When does a shopping trolley (cart) get a little more exciting? When it's a motorcycle!

Boasting a 50 cc engine and revving up to 45 kmh/28 mph, Duncan Everson has built a crazy motorcycle out of a metal shopping cart. The motorized masterpiece was road legal, and Duncan could be seen whizzing past the supermarket in Palmerston North, New Zealand.

"I take it out and cruise around The Square on Friday and Saturday nights. I get a few looks!"

Duncan Everson on his different riding habit

Do It Yourself

To create his unique vehicle, Everson attached a moped engine to the metal frame and then put on wheels from a mower.

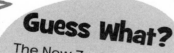

Guess What?

The New Zealand police regularly pull over Everson when he's out on the road to check that his motorized supermarket vehicle is roadworthy.

Lego of Me

Have you ever tried to build a Lego tower? What about one that needs the help of an outdoor crane?

After four days, using 500,000 lego bricks, the folks at Legoland in Windsor, UK, managed to create the world's tallest Lego tower at 29.3 m/96.1 ft. Congratulations all around. However, just months later, another group in Vienna, Austria, broke the world record with a handful more bricks.

Giant Toilet Tissue

In 2007, London, UK, the then longest roll of toilet tissue was unrolled from the world's largest toilet paper holder. The tissue stretched a ridiculous 18.3 km/11.4 miles. Even though it was created for an outdoor stunt, the toilet tissue could be used because it was made by a leading manufacturer.

CHAPTER 3
Extreme Risks

We all like to do things that give us a buzz, like riding a roller coaster or being driven in a superfast car. But for some folks, such pastimes are nowhere near enough. Take a look at a bunch of people who spend their lives searching for the ultimate adrenaline rush.

To Infinity and Beyond

Look up into the skies, and there's a faint chance you'll see a man strapped to a plane wing without the plane!

It may sound like something out of a James Bond film, but this is for real. Yves Rossy broke the world record for being the first person to fly solo across the English Channel strapped to a jet-propelled wing. He made the 35.4 km/22 mile flight in 9 minutes and 7 seconds, moving at an average speed of 200 kmh/124 mph.

> "I fuse with my machine. It was my dream as a boy to be a bird."
> Yves Rossy explaining his passion for flying

Guess What?

Rossy used to fly Mirage fighters for the Swiss army and became an airline pilot. In his spare time, he enjoys parachute jumping. What a surprise!

Stats 'n' Facts

Who: Yves Rossy
Famous for: Flying strapped to a jet-propelled plane wing
Fact: Yves built his world-record-breaking four-jet engine himself in his garage.

Fireball Bus

Flying through the air for 33 m/108 ft over 15 motorcycles in a burning bus isn't for everyone, but Steve Hudis certainly likes it.

A Hollywood stuntman, Hudis pulled off this spectacular fireball feat in 2008. In the process, he inadvertently broke a world record for the longest jump ever by a bus.

Lion King

Lions have big, pointed teeth and are known for biting and eating people, so you'd think lions and children wouldn't mix. Wrong!

Jorge Elich, an eight-year-old boy, became the world's youngest lion tamer in 2008. He is such an expert that he went on to develop his deadly art at the Circus Paris in El Ejido, Spain. His gift for staring into the jaws of death is not new ... he actually started taming lions when he was just five years old!

The Human Spider

Meet the human spider who climbs up the sides of skyscrapers with no safety equipment at all.

Alain "Spiderman" Roberts has been climbing without ropes since he was a child. His first achievement, when he was 12, was scaling eight floors up to his parent's apartment because he had forgotten his keys. Since then, he has earned a world record for the most extreme solo ascent up the Gorge of Verdon in France.

"A city is like a range of mountains with one little difference ... there will always be new skyscrapers under construction."

Death-defying climber, Alain Roberts

Sky-High

The human spider has managed to climb over 70 famous buildings, including the Eiffel Tower in France and the Empire State Building in the USA.

Guess What?

Alain was arrested for climbing the One Houston Center in Texas, USA, without permission. He was only 2 m/6.5 ft off the ground.

39

Wacky Wild Air Race

The Red Bull Air Race World Championships is certainly not for the timid.

The Championship showcases the world's best pilots, who race against the clock around an aerial racetrack marked out by inflatable pylons. They twist and turn approximately 4.5 m/15 ft from the ground at breakneck speeds of 320 kmh/198 mph. The reward? Nothing ... just knowing you're the best!

City to City

The six venues chosen for each round of the 2009 air race were Abu Dhabi, San Diego, Windsor (Canada), Budapest, Porto, and Barcelona.

Guess What?

Planes can safely slice through the pylons that mark the course and continue on their way. They are designed to be as safe as possible.

Stats 'n' Facts

What: Red Bull Air Race
Where: Six different cities
Racetrack length: 5 km/3 miles
Fact: If the pilots clip one of the air pylons with their wings, they receive a 10-second penalty.

Wheel Deal

"Hardcore sitting" is the appropriate label Aaron "Wheelz" Fotherington has given to the extreme stunts he likes to pull in his wheelchair at a US skatepark.

Fotherington pulls the kinds of feats and tricks that would make a professional skateboarder look tame. He is so good that he landed a world record for performing the first-ever backflip in a wheelchair.

"Being in a wheelchair is like carrying your skateboard with you."
Aaron Fotherington, the wheelchair skateboarder

Big Bounce

Aaron's chair is made from a light metal for lightness and strength. It has special super tension to take the impact of hard landings.

Guess What?

The amazing Aaron started using a wheelchair when he was just three. He suffers from a condition known as spina biffida.

41

Horrendous Hobbies

Totally Crazy!

The UK's Thomas Blackthorne is a man of many bizarre hobbies, including eating glass, swallowing razor blades, and sleeping in a pit of snakes.

Perhaps his most spectacular feat has been pushing a giant demolition hammer down his throat and holding it there with no hands for three seconds. The hammer weighed 38 kg/84 lbs, about half the weight of a grown man, so this was no mean feat!

Nine Lives

Alain Roberts, who climbs skyscrapers for fun (see page 39), has had several lucky escapes from death.

In 1982, he fell 15 m/49 ft head first and was in a five-day coma with multiple fractures. Alain recovered, but it left him with vertigo, the condition where you feel unbalanced and dizzy at great heights. Even so, he still climbs.

Just a quick note, folks, to remind you again not to try any of these stunts yourself. Even the experts fail!

Dangerous Sports Club

You may have seen crazy guys on TV pulling risky stunts, but their antics are nothing compared to those of the Dangerous Sports Club.

The UK club was started in the late 1970s by David Kirke and quickly gained risk-loving recruits. Check out just a few of their insane feats below:

★ The world's first-ever modern bungee jump
★ Fying across the English Channel tucked into the pouch of an inflatable kangaroo.

> "A jumbo pilot saw me at 100 feet and assumed it was a UFO."
>
> David Kirke on crossing the English Channel in his helium-filled kangaroo

Being Chased

Alan Weston was chased by a police helicopter in his gorilla outfit before being picked up. His day job now? A rocket scientist for the US Air Force.

Guess What?

Perhaps the club's finest achievement was when Alan Weston flew around the Houses of Parliament in London, UK, in a gorilla outfit playing the saxophone!

Head Over Heels

In August 2006, Travis Pastrana managed to perform the world's first freestyle motocross double backflip on his bike at the fearsome X Games.

The amazing 720 degree flip landed him the highest score ever given by the judges at the Best Trick event. Not surprising when you consider how dangerous the stunt was: Landing incorrectly could have destroyed his career and may have possibly killed him.

"What inspires me and motivates me is someone saying that something can't be done."

Travis Pastrana

Feel the Fear

Travis wasn't sure whether to go ahead with his stunt up until the last minute. He let a game of rock-paper-scissors decide for him!

Guess What?

Travis has stated that he will not be attempting another double backflip. He believes it's up to others to follow in his skid marks.

Buried Alive

Being buried alive in a wooden box is one way of passing the time, but surely it's not the best.

Well, Geoff Smith from Mansfield, UK, might disagree. He was buried alive for nearly five months in a box 1.8 m/5.9 ft long under the ground at his local pub. For company, Geoff had a small TV, personal stereo, mobile (cell) phone, and mini Christmas tree. Yes, he even spent Christmas underground!

"... for the last 30 years, it's been his ambition to go and bury himself in a box."

Hartley Hughes, pub owner

Timely Tribute

Geoff buried himself alive in tribute to his late mother, who clearly wasn't claustrophobic, either. In 1968, she set the original world record of 110 days.

Stats 'n' Facts

Who: Geoff Smith
Famous for: Being buried alive
How long: 147 days
How deep: 1.8 m/5.9 ft
Fact: Geoff breathed through a tube, which was also used to pass food down to him.

Guess What?

In 2004, Zdenek Zahradka from the Czech Republic set a record for being buried alive without food or water when he spent 10 days in a coffin.

When Risks Go Wrong

The Dangerous Sports Club (see page 43) have had many successes, but some of their feats do go wrong.

In 2000, Stella Young was launched 21 m/ 69 ft into the air from a giant catapult. She moved at 80 kmh/50 mph before coming back down to Earth. When she hit the safety net, she bounced out and broke her pelvis. Luckily, optimistic Stella made a speedy recovery.

Human Fireball

Not many people like the idea of being flame-grilled, but it doesn't bother stuntman and daredevil Ted Batchelor.

Totally Crazy!

Ted's top trick is to set himself on fire, walk around, then throw himself off a waterfall to put out the flames. The US human fireball first tried the stunt in 1976 for a bet and has repeated it many times since.

Ted has been burned several times in his career, and what he does is full of danger. Don't try this at home!

Ride the Monster

Do you think surfing a tidal bore wave on a river sounds easy? Well, think again.

Tidal bores are turbulent waves that travel inland against the current. They sweep up rivers at speeds of up to 40 kmh/25 mph. The longest nonstop tidal bore surfing record was set by Brazilian Serginho Laus. He stayed on his board for an incredible 33 minutes and 15 seconds, moving 10.1 km/6.3 miles.

Wild Waves

Tidal bores are known as pororocas in Brazil. This translates as "monster" or "murderer." The locals know how unpredictable these waves are.

"The wave is very powerful and can destroy anything ... trees, local houses, islands."

Serginho Laus on the power of tidal bore waves

Stats 'n' Facts

Who: Serginho Laus
Famous for: Surfing tidal bores
Where: Arguari River, Brazil
Fact: Some tidal bore waves measure up to 9 m/25 ft high and travel up to 300 km/186 miles.

Guess What?

The Qiantang River in China has the most notorious tidal bore in the world. The record for continuous surfing is 1 hour and 10 minutes.

Snow No Fear

Riding a bike down a snow-covered mountain is not recommended, but it will make the bike go very fast!

That's exactly what Austrian Markus Stöckl did to smash the world speed record for series mountain bikes when he careered down a 45-degree icy mountain slope in Chile for 2,000 m/ 6,560 ft. The high-speed run took him 40 seconds to complete, as he moved a staggering 338.7 kmh/210.4 mph.

> "I was very calm. At the end of the course, I had the feeling that I was watching myself riding."
>
> Markus Stöckl on breaking his mountain biking world record

Deep breath!

Markus had to hold his breath for the ride. This was to stop the warmth of his breath steaming up the aerodynamic helmet he was wearing.

Guess What?

Markus beat the previous eight-year-old world record by 22.5 kmh/14 mph. Guess who set that record? He did, of course!

Crazy Bull Run

If you find yourself on the streets of Pamplona, Spain, the second week of July early in the morning, you might want to hide.

This is when the extremely dangerous tradition of the running of the bulls takes place. People dressed in white with red neckerchiefs try to outrun six bulls and two herds of bullocks along an 825 m/2,706 ft course.

It takes only three minutes to complete, but the chances of being trampled or speared in the chest are high.

Tongue Lift

Thomas Blackthorne, the man with the iron throat (see page 42), also has a spectacular tongue.

In July 2007, he set a world record for the heaviest tongue lift by hoisting up an incredible 12 kg/26 lbs of pasta in a glass-walled box. Now, all you geeks out there, go and check the weight of one pack to get an idea of how much pasta that really is!

Stunt Junkie

Travis Pastrana, the motocross backflip hero (see page 44), also enjoys skydiving.

Not so extreme? But he likes to do it without a parachute! In September 2008, the adrenaline junkie leaped from a plane at 3,810 m/12,500 ft minus his essential package. He then glided his way to his jump partner's back and climbed on before his fellow skydiver opened the one parachute between them.

Full-Body Burn

Human fireball Josef Tödtling doesn't just set himself alight, he breaks world records at the same time, too.

In 2013, Josef set the record for the longest full-body burn without an oxygen supply. He managed to stay alight (and alive) for 5 minutes and 41 seconds.

Shocked by the Block

What do you do when being a successful rally driver isn't enough? Well, you could try car jumping stunts instead.

In his spare time, rally driver Ken Block loves to go jumping in state-of the-art cars just for kicks. His most incredible achievement was in 2007 at the New Zealand Snow Park. He pulled off one of the most amazing feats ever by making a huge 21 m/68 ft jump in sync with a pro snowboarder. Cool or what?!

*"I know the physics: 90 miles per hour through trees sideways is pretty d*** scary."*

Ken Block on the danger involved in performing his snow stunt

Stats 'n' Facts

Who: Ken Block
Famous for: Car jump stunts
Stunt vehicle: A Subaru Impressa WRX STi
Fact: Ken is also a joint founder of a successful shoe business.

Guess What?

Ken attempted another jump that was less successful. He overshot the landing ramp and landed his car nose first in the ground.

CHAPTER 4
Incredible People

Some people are born a little different, while others spend a lifetime trying to get themselves noticed. Whatever the case, the world is full of peculiar but incredible people. This section is dedicated to these fearless folk and their amazing attributes.

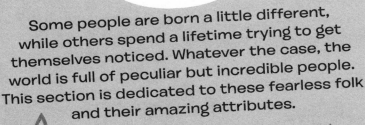

Human Pincushion

Brazilian-born Elaine Davidson is the current world record holder for being the most pierced woman on the planet.

The former nurse, who now lives in Edinburgh, Scotland, was first spotted when she had 462 piercings. Today, she has more than 10,000. Elaine has calculated that all her metal studs and rings together weigh a whopping 3 kg/ 6.6 lbs ... that's like carrying around two whole chickens all the time.

"People often just want to look at me or touch me ... some even want to kiss me!"

Elaine explains people's reactions to her piercings

Metal for Life

Elaine never takes her piercings out. She even goes to bed wearing them. They don't bother her at all, and she sleeps soundly every night.

Stats 'n' Facts

Who: Elaine Davidson
Famous for: Covering her body with metal piercings
Fact: 192 of Elaine's piercings are on her face. It is completely covered with studs and rings!

Guess What?

Elaine loves extremes of all kinds. She enjoys walking on fire, sleeping on a bed of nails, and she has earned herself a black belt in judo in Japan.

Eyes-A-Poppin'

Totally Crazy!

Please don't try this at home, but there are people who can pop their eyeballs almost out of their eye sockets.

American Kim Goodman is one such "eye popper." In 2007, her eyes were measured protruding 12 mm/ 0.47 in out from her face, making her look like a crazy cartoon character. Popping your eyeballs strains the blood vessels and nerves that attach your eyes to your head, so we suggest you leave it to the experts.

Corset Queen

American Cathie Jung has the world's smallest waist, measuring a teeny 38.1 cm/15 in.

To achieve it, Cathie has not gone under the knife. Instead, she has worn corsets pulled tightly day and night for over 25 years. Cathie's husband, a surgeon, believes her corset-wearing does no harm and could help to support her spine rather than damage it.

Bendy Skater Boy

Meet Aniket Chindak, the amazing boy from India who does the splits on roller skates, then whizzes under parked cars.

In 2007, 6-year-old Aniket held the unofficial world record for limbo skating under the most cars in a row. His total was 57 vehicles in 45 seconds. He underwent three months of training before he could even get in the right position!

Top Technique

The trick to skating under so many cars at once is to travel fast enough before bending down into the splits at the last moment.

Stats 'n' Facts

Who: Aniket Chindak
Famous for: Limbo skating under rows of cars
Fact: When Aniket is skating, his body is never more than 20 cm/8 in above the ground.

Guess What?

Aniket trains for up to four hours a day. In a single week, he may travel as much as 97 km/60 miles on his roller skates!

Speed Piercing

Imagine having 1,015 body piercings at once.

That's exactly what Kam Ma did in April 2006 when he and UK-based Charlie Wilson (the piercer) set the world record for the most piercings in a single session. The whole process took 7 hours and 55 minutes. That's a very long time to say "oooooouuuuuch!"

Iceman

How would you like climbing freezing Mount Everest in nothing but your undies?

Well, Wim Hof from Holland doesn't seem to mind. Wim, The Iceman, can withstand temperatures that would prove fatal to the rest of us. He thinks this is due to "Tummo," a form of meditation he uses that allows him to generate heat in any part of his body. Check out his other icy feats:

★ Chilling in a container of ice for over one hour
★ Running a half marathon barefoot in the Arctic.

Hair-Raising Family

The Gomez family is a remarkable one. Many family members suffer from a condition that gives them thick hair all over their bodies, including their faces.

Due to their condition, they had a tough start in life, spending their childhood as part of a sideshow in a cage, where they were known as the "wolf children."

Fortunately, they were rescued by the son of a circus owner and eventually trained in the performing arts.

"I'd never take it off. I am very proud to be who I am."
Larry Ramos Gomez talking about the hair on his body

Acrobatics

Today, brothers Danny and Larry Ramos Gomez perform as acrobats for the Mexican National Circus, where they can show off their skills.

Guess What?

There are about 20 Gomez family members who have the genetic condition that gives them overly hairy bodies. It's known as hypertrichosis.

Super Strength

If you're looking for a pair of rippling biceps, then Georges Christen is your man.

Frenchman Georges is so strong that he doesn't always know his own strength. Once, while admiring a car at a show, he accidentally managed to break off the bumper! However, we can assure you that the feats of strength below were all planned.

★ Ripping up 23 telephone books in two minutes
★ Bending 269 nails in one hour
★ Carrying a woman perched on a table in his teeth for 10 m/32 ft.

"I wanted to be that person the kids were amazed at."

Georges Christen explains why he performs his crazy feats of super strength.

Deep Breath

Georges enjoys blowing up empty hot water bottles, too, just for fun. It takes him a mere 40 seconds to inflate one before it explodes!

Guess What?

Claiming to have set over 20 world records, Georges regularly tours the world with his PowerShow display. It's an unmissable treat.

Tall Story

Bao Xishun never has to worry about reaching the top shelf in the supermarket. That's because he's one of the world's tallest men.

Life hasn't always been easy, though, for the gentle giant. He's in good health, but for many years, he found it hard to find love. However, in 2007, he finally tied the knot with a woman from his town. They are now the proud parents of an average-sized boy!

Stats 'n' Facts

Who: Bao Xishun
Famous for: Being tall
Home: Mongolia
Height: 2.3 m/7 ft 9 in
Fact: Bao is naturally tall. It's not due to a medical condition.

Guess What?

In 2006, Bao saved two dolphins. They had swallowed plastic, which he was able to remove from their stomachs with his extra-long arms.

59

Mr. Muscle

You would have thought that Australian Ray Moon would want to take it easy at the fine age of 87.

But no ... he's a championship bodybuilder.

For the last several years, Ray's been working out for two and half hours up to six days a week. This led to him winning the over–60s division of the Bodybuilding Championships in Melbourne, and he is now believed to be the oldest bodybuilder on the planet.

Tree Man

It began with a single small wart on Dede Koswara's leg and ended with his feet and hands being covered in so many warts that his limbs looked like tree bark.

Dede, from Indonesia, suffers from a condition that stops his body from fighting off the warts. However, since being diagnosed, surgeons have performed four operations to help treat him. Thanks to these, Dede has been able to use his hands again for the first time in 10 years.

Plane Mad

Super-strong Georges Christen (see page 58) has performed one feat that tops them all.

In 1990, he managed to stop three Cessna aircraft from taking off, even though they were cranked up to full power. How? He used his arms to stop two of them from moving and his teeth to hold back the third one!

Tiny Man

Nicknamed "Little Buddha" by his village, Khagendra Magar from Nepal makes a big impression on everyone he meets.

No taller than a preschooler at 67 cm/2 ft 2 in tall, he is the world's shortest "mobile" (able to walk) man. Khagendra has primordial dwarfism. When he was born, he was so tiny that his mother could bathe him while holding him in the palm of her hand.

61

Weirdy Beardies

Totally Crazy!

German Willi Chevalier is just one of a whole bunch of people who love to show off their facial whiskers.

Once every two years, owners of fine facial fur meet for a beard-off at the World Beard and Moustache Championships. In 2007, 252 competitors hit the UK to battle it out in the Moustache, Partial Beard, and Full Beard categories. In each category, there were more classes including Musketeer and Partial Beard Freestyle, which Willi won.

Too Freaky

One competitor in Berlin in 2005 used his beard to recreate the city's famous landmark, the Brandenburg Gate, and included horses and flags!

Stats 'n' Facts

Who: Willi Chevalier
Famous for: Competition-winning facial hair
Class: Partial Beard Freestyle
Fact: Rules state that no hair extensions, hair dye, or hairpins are allowed.

Stuff Your Face

You should eat three meals a day, but American Joey Chestnut seems to have taken this notion a little too far!

He holds several world records for stuffing his face with food. In 2008, Joey entered the Wing Bowl buffalo-wing eating competition in San Jose, California, USA. He managed to chomp his way through 241 of the sticky meaty morsels in 30 minutes flat to secure his record.

"I didn't grow up wanting to do all this. It's something that chose me."

Joey Chestnut on what drives him to eat for fame

Hot Dog!

Joey also holds the world record for wolfing down the most hot dogs in one sitting. He managed 70 of the soggy sausages with buns in just 10 minutes.

Guess What?

A word of warning ... eating like this is not recommended unless you have a burning desire to end up the size of an enormous truck!

Stretch Your Skin

While Gary "Stretch" Turner looks like he is wearing a rubber mask, we can assure you that it's for real.

Gary suffers from a condition called Ehlers-Danlos syndrome, which has left his skin incredibly thin and elastic. Able to pull up his neck skin so that it covers his mouth, he enjoys touring the planet shocking and bedazzling audiences worldwide.

So Licky

Sticking your tongue out may be a fun way of passing the time, but it's not going to make you famous ... unless you're Nick Stoeberl from California, USA.

He measures a whopping 10.1 cm/3.97 in from lip to tip when sticking out, and he holds the official record for the longest tongue in the world. Nick realized he had an abnormally long tongue as a child, and he used to imitate Kiss singer Gene Simmons' famous tongue pose.

The Eating Machine

Totally Crazy!

It took two years for incredible Frenchman Michel Lotito to eat his way through an airplane. Lotito munched the Cessna 150 aircraft between 1978 and 1980. The stunt brought him worldwide media attention and earned him the nickname Monsieur Mangetout (Mr. Eats Everything). His other low-vitamin meals included:

★ 18 bicycles
★ 7 televisions
★ 2 beds
★ 1 coffin.

"We've tried to understand this phenomenon, these antidotes created by his body, but he's basically just a normal guy."

Dr. Bernard Morzol, who studied Mr. Mangetout when he was alive

Guess What?

Mr. Mangetout died in 2006. Doctors assure us it was due to nonmetal-related causes, and his unorthodox diet was not to blame.

Steel Stomach

Lotito's ability to munch up to 900 g/32 oz of metal every day was put down to his stomach lining being twice as thick as a normal person's.

Creepy Cat Man

A pair of fake whiskers wasn't enough for Dennis Enver when he decided to make himself look like a big cat.

A Native American, Dennis had surgery to flatten and upturn his nose. He had fangs like a tiger's inserted into his mouth, and he covered his body in striped tattoos in a bid to turn himself into a tiger. "Stalking Cat," as he is now known, is officially the world's most modified man.

By a Whisker

Dennis also has had his ears lengthened and attachments fitted to his upper lip, so that he can insert cat whiskers.

"I eat meat every day, just as a tiger would. It must be as close to raw as possible."

Stalking Cat talking to a newspaper

Guess What?

Mr. Cat's Native American upbringing inspired him to take on the appearance of his tiger totem symbol. He began changing his body when he was 23.

Stats 'n' Facts

Who: Dennis Enver
Famous for: Looking like a tiger
Name: Stalking Tiger
Fact: When he's not amazing people with his feline looks, Dennis fixes computers.

The Big Breakfast

For breakfast, we don't recommend you following in the footsteps of Luppan Yau.

He managed to polish off five and a half breakfasts at the 2007 All You Can Eat Breakfast Eating Championships in London, UK. The greasy breakfasts included eggs, bacon, sausages, mushrooms, and croissants. Luppan wolfed the whole thing down in an incredible 12 minutes. Indigestion, anyone?

Making a Splash

We all know how painful it can be to belly flop into a swimming pool.

Now, imagine what it must be like for Darren Taylor, aka Profesor Splash, from Denver, Colorado, USA, who regularly sets world records for the highest shallow dive. One feat was a dive from a height of 11 m/36 ft into a mere 30.5 cm/12 in of water!

CHAPTER 5
Peculiar Pastimes

The world is filled with different creeds, heritages, and cultures. But we're all the same when you get right down to it: We all love laughing at our own ridiculousness. So enjoy the freedom over the next few pages, and be inspired. Maybe you will dream up your own peculiar pastime!

Canonball Superstars

It makes for an interesting discussion around the family dinner table: "Dad, what are you doing today?" Reply: "Well, I'm firing myself out of a cannon."

David "Cannonball" Smith, Sr. made his name by being shot distances of more than 50 m/165 ft in the 1990s. The rest of the family, including his sister and his son, are following in his footsteps.

Blast Off

David still enjoys a blast in between making cannons for other family members. He even shot himself over the USA-Mexican border.

Guess What?

The Smiths' act is no walk in the park and requires lots of planning. Once out of the cannon, you must keep your body totally straight at all times.

Stats 'n' Facts

Who: David Smith, Sr.
Famous for: Touring the world as a human cannonball
Top speed: 112 kmh/70 mph
Fact: You can expect to experience a g-force of 11 ... that's 11 times your body weight.

Air Guitar Hero

Want to experience the thrill of being a guitar hero without actually having to learn to play the guitar? Then this is your moment.

The Air Guitar World Championships are held in Finland each year. Competitors show off their skills to two song snippets: one selected by the organizers and one of their own choosing. Body movement and ludicrous facial expressions are crucial to an amazing performance, but no real instruments are ever allowed.

> "It's impossible to be angry and play air guitar."
>
> Zac Monro, Air Guitar World Champion 2001 and 2002

Guess What?

Top tracks selected by the organizers for you to air guitar to include Nirvana's *Smells Like Teen Spirit* and Green Day's *American Idiot*.

Hard Rock

You can choose to rock out on an imaginary electric guitar or show your sensitive side on an acoustic. You may even use a real guitar pick for added effect.

Jets for Thrills

Michel Pont has an expensive but exciting hobby: He collects jet fighter planes.

Since 1985, Michel has owned the biggest private collection of jet fighters in the world. The planes are kept on his 16 ha/40 acre vineyard in France. But that's not the end of the story. If Michel ever gets bored with his impressive aircraft collection, he can always take a spin in one of 300 motorcycles or 34 Abarth Fiat race cars, which he also owns.

On View

If you would like to see Michel Pont's epic collection of planes, motorcycles, and cars, they are on display in the museum at his French chateau.

Stats 'n' Facts

Who: Michel Pont
Pastime: Collecting jet fighters
Number in collection: 110
Fact: When Michel isn't admiring his planes, you can find him working at his day job as a wine maker.

Guess What?

Michel is unable to take off in any of his planes from his huge vineyard because the fighters are banned from use in French airspace.

Cheesy Run

Totally Crazy!

Every year, crowds gather at Cooper's Hill in the UK to watch crazy folk roll down a hill in pursuit of a lump of cheese in one of the world's zaniest events.

There are five races. For each one, up to 20 people get ready at the top of the mega steep hill before the cheese is released. Once it's rolling, the competitors follow it down the near-vertical slope. Whoever reaches the bottom first is the winner and gets to keep the cheese.

Cheese Wheel

A delicious 3.2 kg/7 lb ball of Double Gloucester cheese is used for the event. The circular cheese can reach speeds of up to 112 kmh/70 mph.

"My god! It's not a hill; it's a cliff. People throw themselves down a cliff, after some cheese."
First-time cheese roller, Chris Hodgkins

Guess What?

Don't think you are safe hanging with the crowd. Both competitors and runaway balls of cheese sometimes roll off into the masses.

Stats 'n' Facts

Event: Cheese rolling
Where: Gloucestershire, UK
How it works: You roll down a slope chasing a ball of cheese.
Fact: Running is allowed, but it's safer to slide or roll because the slope is so steep.

Meet the Ninjas

A Ninja festival is held every April in Japan with up to 30,000 spectators. Many come dressed for the part.

During the festival, people can be seen clutching maps and walking the streets, as they hunt out hidden life-sized Ninja mannequins placed around the city. Families often wear the full costume of the stealth warrior, including his 'n' hers matching swords.

It's a Secret

You can learn more about the Ninja's secret ways in the Igaryu Ninja museum, which boasts a residence with revolving walls and secret trapdoors.

Stats 'n' Facts

Event: Ninja festival
Where: Iga, Japan
How it works: Dress Ninja, and celebrate this ancient art.
Fact: It is thought that Ninjas wore dark blue rather than black to hide in the moonlight.

Guess What?

Ninjas were prepared at all times. At night, Ninjas would always lie on their left sides to protect their hearts from sudden knife attacks.

New Year Soaker

Want a water fight? Then head straight to Thailand in the middle of April.

Once a year, Thai people take to the streets armed with water pistols, buckets of water, and the odd elephant to douse residents and tourists alike with sprays of glorious H_2O. This is how the Thai people celebrate Songkran, the official start of the Buddhist New Year.

Canonball Disaster

The Smith family (see page 69) are not the only people who are partial to being shot through the air at ridiculously high speeds. Todd Christian is, too.

However, things haven't worked out quite so well for British Todd. Although he doesn't mind being a human cannonball, he has a fear of flying. So, when asked to take a long-haul flight to Brazil for a specialist training course, he refused. The result? He was fired from his job. Excuse the pun!

Big Tomato Splat Fest

It's the world's best food fight, and everyone is invited!

To start the fight, which takes place in Buñol, Spain, one person from a vast crowd scrambles up a greasy pole and grabs the leg of ham at the top. More than 40,000 people then start pelting each other with tomatoes. Known as La Tomatina, the seriously squishy splat fest takes place every year.

"Never, and we mean never, climb on a gate, window, wall, etc. to be able to watch the battle. You will become the target of 40,000 people."

The golden rule given on the event's website

Tomato War

It's claimed that the first tomato war started in 1945 when a fight broke out between local youths, who grabbed the tomatoes from a market stall.

Guess What?

Originally, the tomato fight was banned, but in 1955, people marched through the streets with a coffin containing a tomato to get the ban lifted.

Gurn and Bear It

What is gurning, and why do people do it? The answer to the first question is: It's the art of pulling faces. The answer to the second question is: Who knows?

What we do know is that Briton Tommy "Quasimodo" Mattinson won the World Gurning Championships 14 times between 1986 and 2012 and earned himself a rightful place in the record books.

"Don't stay like that for too long, or your face will stay like that."
UK Prince Philip to Tommy Mattinson, Gurning World Champion

Wrinkle Up

For the competition, Tommy had to put his head through a horse's collar and scrunch up his face into the most revolting poses imaginable.

Stats 'n' Facts

Event: Gurning Championship
How it works: You pull the most hideous face you can manage.
Where: Cumbria, UK
Fact: Held at the Egremont Crab Fair, the competition has now become world famous.

Bog Snorkel

Totally Crazy!

It's best not to get too bogged down with this particular preposterous pastime.

The World Bog Snorkelling Championships take place once a year just outside Llanwrtyd, Wales. The premise is simple. Two 55 m/180 ft trenches are dug, and contestants are then required to swim down them with flippers and a snorkel, fancy hats allowed. Whoever gets to the end first is the winner.

A Tad Stinky

The water in the trenches has been described as being like pea soup; the smell is bad. Watch out for the odd newt you might swallow as well!

Stats 'n' Facts

Event: Bog snorkel competition
How it works: Swim through a mud pool with a snorkel.
Where: Llanwrtyd, Wales
Fact: Regular swimming techniques are not encouraged.

Guess What?

The sludgy event has been attracting people for more than 20 years. People put themselves through this trench warfare in the name of charity.

Crazy English

The "Elvis of English" is how Li Yang has been described for his remarkable Crazy English classes.

Chinese Li doesn't give normal classroom-based lessons like a crusty old teacher. No, Li likes to get on stage and teach crowds of 50,000 people at the same time. His technique? To get the audience to shout out the words while pulling an expressive face and gesturing wildly. It really works!

Slippery Pole

Becoming a winner at the annual Independence Day celebrations in Indonesia is a slippery affair.

In the competition, people climb up an oil-coated tree while fellow competitors try to pull them back down to get ahead themselves. Jeans, in particular, are at risk of being lost! But it's all worth it for the prizes at the top of the poles, which may include a bicycle, keys to a brand new motorcycle, and ... uh ... a plastic bucket.

Wife Wars

Sometimes love can become a drag ... literally!

Created in Finland, the Wife Carrying Championship started out as a little joke back in 1992, but since then, the craze has swept the planet. The United States, China, the UK, Italy, and Australia all enter, with competitors slinging wives over their backs in a 253 m/ 830 ft assault course.

> *"The wives and the wife carriers are not afraid of challenges or burdens."*
>
> From the Wife Carrying Championship's official website

Heave-Ho

The challenging course features two obstacles that competitors need to heave themselves over and also a water obstacle that they wade through.

Stats 'n' Facts

Event: Wife-carrying race
How it works: Men run with a woman flung over their shoulder.
Where: Sonkajärvi, Finland
Fact: One rule is that wives must be over 17 years old.

Guess What?

This race is serious, and there are several golden rules, including one that says all participants must have fun ... even if they fall on their faces!

Incredible Human Tower

Head to Tarragona, Spain, if you ever have the urge to build a human tower.

The famous Castells Competition takes place every two years in the city's bull-fighting ring, where entrants gather to build the highest human tower. The base is created by a mass of heavy-set people, with smaller groups leaping up to create the next stages. Children are often used at the top because they are light.

Crazy Origami

The amazing Hawaiian, Won Park, spends his time creating origami figures from the humble US dollar.

Won, a paper-folding expert, has recreated scenes from *Star Wars* and *Star Trek* through to a jumping frog and a toilet with its own lid. He can make just about any object, and he insists that he never uses glue, tape, or scissor cuts of any kind.

Big Crybaby

Totally! Crazy!

At the Crying Sumo competition in Japan, screaming babies are positively encouraged.

Every year, babies born in the area are brought to the Senso-ji temple to compete in a crying contest. Each baby is held by a student sumo wrestler and coaxed into bawling by the students and a temple priest, who waves his arms around. If this doesn't work, the wrestlers put on their scary masks. That usually does the trick!

"... Crying Sumo is held to pray for children's healthy growth."
From a report by the *Mainichi Daily News*

Scream Loud

The competition winner is the baby that bawls first. If both start to howl at the same time, then the loudest screamer takes the trophy.

Stats 'n' Facts

Event: Crying Sumo competition
How it works: You bring a baby and hope it screams its head off.
Where: Tokyo, Japan
Fact: Sumos are allowed to raise the baby above their heads to encourage howling.

The Vikings Are Back

For one night a year in January, the Scottish bring back the Vikings and run riot through the town.

At the Up Helly Aa Festival, you can watch astonishing scenes of grown men dressed in Viking costumes with horned helmets march through the streets of Lerwick, Scotland, dragging a 9 m/29 ft replica longboat behind them. If that's not impressive enough, they're followed by 900 more people in various disguises carrying fiery torches.

Let It Burn!

The festival's highlight is the burning of the longboat to music and fireworks, followed by an evening of drinking the Vikings would be proud of!

Stats 'n' Facts

Event: Up Helly Aa Festival
How it works: You dress up as a Viking and drag a boat along.
Where: Shetland Isles, Scotland
Fact: Up Helly Aa is the biggest fire festival in Europe.

Guess What?

Up Helly Aa takes place to celebrate the arrival of the Vikings over 1,000 years ago. The horned ones ruled parts of Scotland for 600 years.

Owl Stash

American Pam Barker got more than she bargained for when she replied to an ad for a motley collection of furry and china owls.

In the ad, it stated there were 14,000 pieces of owl memorabilia up for sale, but Pam thought this was a mistake and that 1,400 was a more realistic figure. However, it was true, and Pam got landed with the massive stash of owls.

Let that be a lesson to any collectors out there!

"My husband would like his store back."

Pam Barker on how her collection lives in her partner's building supplies store

Guess What?

Pam bought her owls after their previous owner died. In tribute, Pam left the previous owner's name in the record books rather than her own.

It's a Record

In 2006, Pam held the biggest collection of owl memorabilia in the world. She was usurped in 2016 by Israeli Yaakov Chai, who collected 19,100.

CHAPTER 6
Weird Sports

For some sports, you need to be more than just awesome ... you need to be mad as a hatter as well! So no matter what your shape or size is, you, too, can become a competition-slaying super sports hero because there is a weird sport out there for just about everybody.

Redneck Olympics

Y'all come on down! Welcome to the Redneck Games, which features the silliest sports in the entire United States.

Started in 1996 as a small event to entertain the locals and gently mock the Olympic Games being held up the road in Atlanta, the Redneck Games has become an institution attracting thousands of people.

Wacky events included:

★ Seeing how far you can throw a hubcap

★ Throwing yourself into a garbage can to find a prize

★ Showing how far you can spit a seed.

"All profit ... every last cent ... from the Redneck Games goes to local charities. We don't make a dime ... That's not what it's about."

Mac Davis, creator of the Redneck Games

Guess What?

Don't expect to win a gold medal at the Redneck Games. The prize for most events is a trophy with a crushed beer can at the top.

Big Bungee Jump

Why do a bungee jump on your own when you can hang off a cord upside down with 25 others?

This mass jump of crazy men and women was performed in 1998 in front of the Deutsche Bank headquarters in Germany. The tightly packed group plummeted 52 m/170 ft before bouncing back up again. It's unofficially the world's biggest mass jump. Let's hope they didn't eat lunch beforehand!

Tweed Run

The next time you're in central London, UK, keep your eyes peeled for a bunch of guys (well, mainly) on vintage bicycles dressed from head to toe in tweed.

Since 2009, the London single speed and fixed gear cycling forum has welcomed cyclists on a leisurely but stylish jaunt past the capital's finest sites, with a cup of tea in the park. The rules are simple ... Harris tweed suits, plus fours, and an antique bike!

Totally Crazy! Feathered Speed Fiends

Flightless ostriches might look a little gangly and useless, but these mighty birds can run like the wind.

They're also seriously dangerous and aggressive, but that doesn't seem to stop people in some countries from wanting to climb on their backs and race them as fast as they can down a track!

> "An ostrich that hasn't been worked with can be very cantankerous. They can kill you."
>
> Joe Hedrick, ostrich expert, explains the perils of working with these birds

Guess What?

A riderless ostrich has a top speed of 64 kmh/40 mph. It can outrun a racehorse. A human has absolutely no chance of keeping up.

Get Set, Go!

At Highgate Ostrich Farm in South Africa, ostrich racing is a daily event for the farm workers. Spectators are always kept a safe distance away.

Swinging on the Wing

Enter the Swing on Wing golfing tournament, and you're in for a little bit more than gentle shots on the green.

For this crazy competition, held in Abu Dhabi in the United Arab Emirates, you need to balance on the wing of a parked airplane and whack the ball with your club as far as you can. Let's just hope driving wind and rain aren't predicted on the day!

Donkey Challenge

They may not look like the world's purest thoroughbreds, but donkey racing is massively popular.

That includes kids having fun in donkey derbys in the UK, Santas (yes, really!) racing donkeys at festivals in the Swiss Alps, and professional jockeys in Germany galloping around a track for prize money. It sounds incredible, but one racing donkey was sold for £25,000 ($32,000).

Rock-Paper-Scissors

While you might think of the game rock-paper-scissors as a way to pass the time, some people believe it is a full-blown sport.

Sean Sears won serious prize money in the Bud Light USA Rock Paper Scissors League Tournament in 2008. But his ultimate challenge was the international championship in China. He managed a respectable bronze, losing out to rock-paper scissors supremo, Mark Cleland, who took gold.

"Facing off against the finest rock-paper-scissors players in the world was an intense challenge ... "

Mark Cleland, International Rock Paper Scissors champion

Your Arsenal

There is a version of this game that features 22 different objects, including guns, lightning, axes, fire, snakes, and even nuclear weapons!

Stats 'n' Facts

Sport: Rock-paper-scissors
How it works: You make weapon shapes with your hand.
Prize money: US $50,000
Fact: The "sport" is so popular in the USA, it's even televised.

Guess What?

Some players include dynamite in the game. But there is a dispute that paper could beat dynamite by covering the wick on the stick.

Seriously Crazy Soccer

The Brits are bonkers about soccer, so this must explain why they play the ever-so-scary Shrovetide Football (Soccer) Match once a year in Ashbourne, Derbyshire.

Known as the "no rules" game, two teams made up of people from opposite ends of the town play a match where each team's goalposts are 5 km/3 miles apart. The game boasts hundreds of players and takes two days. Each half game lasts a punishing eight hours.

Stats 'n' Facts

Sport: Weird soccer
How it works: It's played with no rules and as many people as possible on a team.
Fact: There is just one rule: You're not allowed to murder anyone!

It's a Goal!

To score a goal in this crazy game, you need to hit the ball three times against a specially built plinth that has a millstone on top of it.

Guess What?

The game is thought to be 1,000 years old. Some people think that it used to be played with a severed head rather than a soccer ball!

I Say, How Spiffing, Old Chap!

Totally Crazy!

If you're tired of bad manners and crude habits, you could always take part in the Chap Olympics. Founders Gustav Temple and Torquil Arbuthnot, who also run *The Chap* magazine, have created a UK-based event to act as a shining beacon to proper conduct. So once a year, folks turn up in their finest suits and dresses to indulge in silly sports, including:

★ Three-trousered limbo
★ Pipe smoker's relay race
★ Cucumber sandwich, discuss
★ Lobster "moustache" duel.

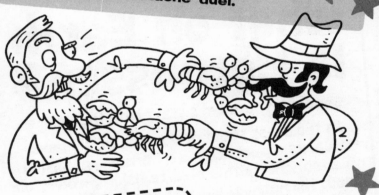

Stats 'n' Facts

Sport: Chap Olympics
How it works: You do silly things politely while dressed in suits.
Fact: Gustav Temple suggests white shoes for all events.

Silly Sport

The lobster "moustache" duel works exactly as it says. Two contestants attack each other's moustaches and beards with lobsters. I say!

Armpit Serenade

Are you a master of armpit farting? If so, you may want to take a trip to the Redneck Games (see page 85), where this is one of the crazy games. The aim is to create the loudest, boldest fart by cupping your hand under your armpit and flapping your elbow up and down like a mad chicken. If you can play a well-known tune as well, you're guaranteed to win!

What on Earth Is Hornussen?

Good question! Let's start with the basics.

In the Swiss sport of Hornussen, a player thwacks a puck, called a hornuss, mounted on a launcher with a bizarre fishing–rod–style club. The hornuss whizzes through the air at up to 320 kmh/199 mph toward the opposing team. They are holding schindels (wooden placards), and the aim is to catch the flying hornuss without injuring yourself. Get it? No, we don't either!

Get Moooving

Forget the elegant sport of horse racing. No, we're more interested in water buffalo racing.

At the heart of the annual water buffalo festival in Chonburi, Thailand, is a buffalo race on a drag strip 100 m/330 ft long. Riders storm down the course, clinging on for dear life without stirrups or saddle, and hope they'll get to the end before the animal decides to do its own thing and not finish, or they fall off.

Stats 'n' Facts

Sport: Water buffalo racing
How it works: You climb on a water buffalo with no saddle.
Where: Chonburi, Thailand
Fact: Some water buffalo are now bred purely for racing.

Guess What?

In the past, the buffalo also worked the fields for the rice harvest. Locals believed that racing the buffalo made them work quicker.

Buffalo Fight

Some people say that water buffalo racing started because two farmers got into an argument about whose buffalo could run the fastest.

By George, It's Bounders!

Here's yet another wacky game from the impeccably dressed contestants at the Chap Olympics (see page 91).

In Bounders, six chaps are given two minutes to behave appallingly to six ladies. Once suitably offended, the ladies must slap the chaps. The cad on the receiving end of the loudest slap is declared the winner. Yes, those chaps really are that nutty!

Is It a Bird or a Plane?

Totally Crazy!

No, it's Bognor Birdman, actually, one of the many people who come to the seaside town of Bognor Regis in the UK to throw themselves off a pier.

Contestants turn up with bizarre flying contraptions to see how far they can get. Many devices are just plain ridiculous, such as flying hedgehogs or toilets, but a few committed engineers arrive with incredible homemade gliders that can travel spectacular distances.

Horse Versus Human

Llanwrtyd Wells in Wales is not only famous for people who like to bog snorkel (see page 77), it is also the starting point for a marathon where humans compete against horses.

You would expect the horses to win every time, but in a surprising turn of events in 2007, two lightning-fast runners beat the cantering ponies and their riders.

The horse camp blamed the very hot weather for the defeat. What a night-mare!

Muddy Belly Flop

Feel like throwing yourself face first into a pit of mud? Well, head off to the Redneck Games (see page 85).

"The fatter, the better" is the one rule to follow in this seriously sticky event as the contestant's flabby bellies help them to make a big impact in the mud pool. Winners are judged on belly-flopping style and the size of the splash they make.

Boxing Clever

Chess boxing sees two extemely clever fighters alternating between punching each other and sitting down in the ring for a game of chess.

At the amazing World Chess Boxing Championships, there are a total of 11 rounds ... six rounds of chess and five rounds of fisticuffs. If no one is knocked out or has declared "checkmate" after all the rounds, the fight is decided on the points earned during the boxing bouts.

"One minute you're having your skull battered, the next you're sat down trying to work out why you appear to have 48 pawns."

Ringside report, Georgina Turner

How Unfair!

If there is a tie at the end of the boxing match, the person in control of the black pieces on the chess board is the winner. Hardly fair!

Guess What?

The first Chess Boxing Light Heavyweight Championship took place in Berlin in 2007. It was won by German Frank Stoldt, gloves down.

Rolling Down the Road

Irish road bowling is perhaps the cheapest sport known to humans.

This event sees competitors hurling a 0.8 kg/1.7 lb iron ball down a closed-off public road. Whoever completes the 4 km/2.5 mile course with the fewest throws is declared the winner. It's hugely popular in Ireland, with large crowds gathering to watch. Just be careful not to get a huge ball of iron in your face!

Toilet Seat Throwing

Totally Crazy!

Any sport involving toilet seats could only be part of the Redneck Games (see page 85). Here's how it works ...

Take one lightweight plastic toilet seat, and cross your fingers that it's clean. Now, throw it carefully, aiming for a stake in the ground. Did we say a stake? We meant a toilet plunger, of course! The person who lands the seat over the plunger handle wins.

Get Set ... Glug, Glug

Hearing the firing pistol must have been one of the easier things to do at the Underwater Olympics.

In 2008, Qiando Underwater World in China decided to beat Beijing at its own games by holding a special underwater sporting event. Dressed in wet suits and laden with scuba gear, divers undertook various events. These included:

★ Hurdles in a wet suit
★ Fencing with an oxygen tank
★ Watery gymnastics.

Tricky Target

Life was made difficult for divers in the shooting event. They had to stand on a wire while trying to hit an inflated balloon 5 m/16 ft away.

Guess What?

Not to be outdone, Coex Aquarium in South Korea held their own underwater Olympics. It included underwater soccer and tae kwon do.

Stats 'n' Facts

Sport: Underwater Olympics
How it works: Like the normal Olympics but with scuba gear
Where: China, South Korea
Fact: Spectators watch under the water behind a glass wall.

Ironing Man

Totally Crazy!

Well, if you're going to iron your jeans, why not do it up the side of a mountain?

Created by Phil Shaw, the first Extreme Ironing World Championship for daredevils with a passion for pristine clothes took place in Germany in 2002. Competitors had to grab clothes, irons, and ironing boards, then iron in a series of bizarre places: up a tree, down a river, and while climbing a wall.

> "... they forget the main reason they are there in the first place: to rid their clothing of creases and wrinkles."
>
> Phil Shaw on competitors' obsession with dangerous locations

Not Boring!

Shaw came up with the idea of extreme ironing when doing the laundry at home. He decided he needed to find a way to make the task less boring.

Guess What?

The sport of extreme ironing faces some stiff competition from the Urban Housework group, who have started downhill vacuuming!

99

Cow Dung Golf

The Swiss are not normally known for their frivolity, but judging from the Cow Dung Golf Tournament, they're starting to let their hair down.

Now in its third successful year, this smelly sport has competitors marching up the Swiss Alps to see who can hit the most piles of poo with a golf club in two hours. Just imagine the stinky mess at the end!

All Out Wall

It's a crazy sport for upper-crust English people only, so count yourself lucky!

Known as the Eton Wall game, this sport is played only by boys who attend Eton College in the UK. Players are split into two teams and head to a long wall at the school. Then they battle it out, trying to get the ball from one end of the wall to the other by using their feet and piling into one another. It's hardly gentlemanly!

Let's Get Mowing

If you're not rich enough to indulge in Formula One racing, you could always hop on a mower instead.

The British Lawnmower Racing Association boasts four different classes for potential racers, including everything from hand-pushed models to wheel-based mowers that can achieve speeds of up to 80 km/50 mph. The event lasts for 12 hours, with riders pushing or riding their mowers late into the night.

Race for It

For the British Lawnmower Racing Association's 25th anniversary in 1997, competitors raced nonstop for 25 hours instead of the usual 12 hours.

Stats 'n' Facts

Sport: Mower racing
How it works: You find an old or new mower and whizz it around a track as fast as possible.
Where: UK
Fact: The race is an incredible 482 km/300 miles long.

Guess What?

Fans of mower racing past and present have included the British actor Oliver Reed and car racing legend, Sterling Moss.

101

CHAPTER 7
Groups Go Crazy

They say that people have strength in numbers. Well, judging by this chapter, it simply gives people more of a excuse to behave like total lunatics. Nothing wrong with that, of course. Perhaps, we should take a leaf out of their books and go a little crazy with our friends once in a while!

Laugh Off Your Troubles

Feeling down? Then take part in World Laughter Day, an event designed to giggle away your blues.

At the heart of all this hilarity is the "Guru of Giggling," Dr. Madan Kataria, who created Laughter Yoga in 1995. It proved so successful that he has now taught people the principles of laughter therapy in over 60 countries, and there are over 6,000 laughter clubs worldwide.

Guess What?

Policemen in Allahbad, India, use laughter therapy at the beginning of their taxing day to help lift their spirits. You could try, too!

Stats 'n' Facts

Event: World Laughter Day
How it works: You start laughing and try to infect everyone else.
When: First Sunday in May
Where: Worldwide
Fact: Laughing can bring down your stress and anxiety levels.

How to Laugh

There is a technique to induce laughter. In a group, start off by faking the laughter. In time, it will become real because chuckling is so infectious.

Swimming Club

When most people go swimming, they prefer an empty pool with plenty of room to work on their swimming strokes.

Not in China, though. They pack themselves in like sardines! Temperatures can get so high in Sichuan province that locals rush to the nearest pool to escape the heat. There's no chance of swimming, though. The pools gets so jammed that all you can do is stand there. Let's just hope that no one needs the bathroom!

I Gave My Heart to a Stormtrooper

The 501st Legion is planet Earth's biggest group of dedicated *Star Wars* fans.

There are over 3,300 members from 30 countries, and they like to come together to dress up in stormtrooper costumes. In 2007, 200 members marched down the streets of Pasadena, California, USA, fully decked out to raise money for charity. George Lucas, the creator of the film series, was in attendance and full of praise.

Beef on the BBQ

The people of Paraguay must have eyes bigger than their bellies because they are the record holders of the world's largest one-day open-air barbecue.

Over 30,000 people wolfed down an astonishing 28,000 kg/61,729 lb of beef in six hours. Alas though, not everyone was happy. Some people complained that there wasn't enough to eat! It seems you can't please all of the people all of the time ...

> "It's the largest quantity of meat that has been eaten at one event in one day."
> Ralph Hannah, judge at the world's biggest barbecue

Nice Name

The event's name was "Todo bicho que camina va al asador." For those who are not linguists, that means "Every critter walking goes to the barbecue."

Gues

The
barl
of
Bay
i

Winged Wonders

Flying in formation with just a few skydivers takes skill and practice, so free-falling through the air with 71 people en masse is almost unbelievable.

It took five days of solid practice for the skydiving teams to set an unofficial record. The team jumped an incredible 30 times over Lake Elsinore, California, USA, before they decided they were ready to try officially. Luckily, they did the job!

"Our biggest concern is a collision in the sky. _collision in the sky_ _knock you out_ _our bones._"

fore the _ing_

Whizzing By

es were used in the record carrying a team of skydivers vn to the ground at speeds kmh/100 mph.

W
Fa
tow

s What?

world's long
becue was
by the p
amband
n 2014
a whopp
20.246

s What?

skydivers
r amazing
re was only
separating
ne before
pened their
rachutes.

Mad about Games

DreamHack in Jönköping, Sweden, is the largest computer gaming party in the world. More than 27,000 participants gather to play games like Counter-Strike, Super Smash Bros, and Dota 2 over a local network.

Over 50,000 gaming fans from all over the world visited DreamHack in 2016, which also included cosplay and live concerts.

Cat Crew

The city of Kuching, Malaysia, is said to have been named after the Malay word for "cat." So in a city filled with cat statues and a cat museum, it was only fitting that the feline-friendly people of Kuching met in 2017 to become the world's largest gathering of people dressed as cats.

A minimum of 250 people in full-feline attire were required to break the previous record. Over 440 paw-sitive cat lovers turned up to make this a purr-fectly memorable record.

Jedi Gym Class

Ever wanted a workout with a difference? Well, the Ludosport Light Saber Combat Academy in Milan, Italy, offers just that.

People flock to the Jedi Academy to learn seven different styles of Jedi combat. As well as brushing up on how to brandish a light saber without putting your eye out, you also learn how to stop Darth Maul with a throw.

Weird Whispers

You'd think that passing a simple message down a line of people might be easy, but it's not so!

A group of British children set a new world record for the longest game of Chinese Whispers. To raise money for charity, 1,330 children gathered in a London football stadium to pass on the message: "Together we will make a world of difference." This eventually changed to "everyone is evil," and after two hours, it was just "haaaaa." We recommend email!

City of Angels

Los Angeles has been upstaged as the City of Angels by the city of Bismarck, North Dakota, USA.

In December 2007, Bismarck's residents turned up to make 8,962 snow angels. To do this, they all threw themselves on their backs at the same time and waved their arms around. It looked extremely silly, but it was a matter of pride, and it gave the city a world record.

"It's fun and puts us on the map. People think there's nothing going on up here."
Bismarck resident, to the Associated Press

Angel Basics

To make the perfect snow angel, lie in the snow, and move as if you're doing a star jump. Then, get up and look at the lovely shape you've left behind.

Guess What?

Everyone got involved. The youngest snow angel was a six-week-old baby, and the oldest was 99-year-old Pauline Jaeger.

Leap for Your Country

Want to show your patriotism? Then why not throw yourself out of a plane in the shape of a flag?

That's exactly what 200 Germans did in 2008 to set a new world record for the most Germans free-falling at the same time. With this crazy stunt, they managed to beat the previous record of 156 Germans leaping for their country. Wearing suits in the shades of the German flag, it was truly an impressive sight.

Drink the Bath Water

If your parents are moaning about being stressed, you could recommend the Yunessun Spa in Japan.

In 2009, guests at the resort enjoyed the delights of bathing in a pool filled to the brim with red wine. Staff were on hand to pour glasses of wine for those who couldn't get enough of the booze and were tempted to drink directly from the pool itself!

Stiletto Sprint

Some women love their stilettos, even when they are running in them.

Witness the bizarre site of 265 Australian women racing each other in Sydney around an 80 m/262 ft course to break a world record. The winner, Brittney McGlone, was the first to make it to the end of what must have been a torturous experience for everyone involved.

> "About six girls in front of me fell, and two or three heels started spiking up at me."
>
> One competitor, talking to Australia's *Daily Telegraph* before showing her injury

Heel Rules

The rules stated that runners had to wear 7.6 cm/3 in heels. Smooth legs were also required, so painful waxing was needed.

Stats 'n' Facts

Event: Stiletto sprinting
How it works: You run as fast as you can in high heels ... ouch!
Where: Sydney, Australia
Fact: A few men were also spotted racing in high heels.

Guess What?

Holland held the previous record for stiletto sprinting. Only 150 women were unfortunate enough to run wearing the deadly footwear.

Weird Science

OK, here's a "scientific" experiment for you. Just make sure you do it in the open air with plenty of space around you and your parents on standby!

★ Take one large bottle of diet cola.
★ Now drop one or more Mentos™ mints into it.
★ Keep your head away to avoid a black eye, and watch the drink explode out of the bottle in a fizzy fountain.

This trick is all the rage with students in Riga, Latvia. They set off an amazing 1,911 sickly sweet geysers at the same time to bag a world record in 2008.

Mint Theory

Why does the drink explode? One theory is that the pores in the sweets soak up the carbon dioxide in the cola, causing the fountain to erupt.

Guess What?

Reports say that eating Mentos™ after drinking diet cola can be fatal. No one has died yet, but we suggest you do NOT try to find out!

Strictly Scuba

Totally Crazy!

Seventy-four scuba divers standing at the bottom of a pool sounds like a crowd in need of an open ocean.

But there was a reason for this extreme gathering: They were all taking a dance class while trying to keep in sequence for over 10 minutes. The crazy flipper-footed Australians managed to do just that and set a world record in the process.

Game Crazy

Zelda, Mario, and Sonic are just a few of the popular characters of the video gaming world who all got together in real life in 2008.

A huge group of British fans dressed up as video game characters and headed off to the London Games Festival in the UK. There were 342 of the crazy characters, which gave them a world record for the most fans dressed as video game characters gathered together in one place at the same time.

CHAPTER 8
Totally Bizarre

It's hard to imagine why some people do what they do. Their ideas and achievements are so wacky that you wonder how they came up with them in the first place. So we've rounded up and captured the following "out there" madcap items to form this eccentric section.

Freak School

Forget trawling through the works of Shakespeare. For a truly unique education, sign up to the Coney Island Sideshow School in New York, USA.

Here, you can learn how to be a circus performer in seven days, including: the art of sword swallowing, fire breathing, and escaping from a straitjacket while hanging upside down. Oh, and study how to hammer a spike into your head without dying instantly.

Sick Name

The teacher who runs the week-long course is the charmingly named Donny Vomit. He's been tossing chainsaws for well over a decade now.

Guess What?

According to Donny, there are three kinds of freaks: natural, man-made, and working. If you learn a skill to perform, that makes you a working freak.

"Be a freak in just one week!"
The Coney Island Sideshow School motto

Peculiar Protestor

If you're a protester and a performance artist, then you've got to do a little more to stand out from the crowd. Brit Mark McGowan is just that. Here are a few of his peculiar stunts:

★ Sitting in a bath full of beans to protest against the negativity surrounding the great British fried breakfast

★ Crawling 88 km/55 miles looking for love with a box of chocolates tied to his body and a rose in his mouth

★ "Sailing" from London to Glasgow in a shopping "trolley" (that's "cart" in the USA!) to improve relations between England and Scotland.

"I pushed a monkey nut (peanut in a shell) for seven miles with my nose, from New Cross all the way to 10 Downing Street. I was protesting against student debt."

Mark McGowan on one of his headline-grabbing protest stunts

Sail Failed

Mark's shopping trolley trip ended in disaster after less than a quarter of the journey. He had to give up due to poor weather conditions.

Guess What?

Mark tried to cartwheel from London to Brighton, UK, with rocks strapped to his feet in protest at people taking pebbles from Brighton beach.

Human Lamp

Totally Crazy!

Zhang Deke makes the ideal guest if you're having trouble with your lights.

The highway maintenance man from China likes nothing better than charging his body up with 220 volts of electricity, then placing light bulbs on his head and ears, and lighting them up. Zhang is also able to cook fish on his abdomen in two minutes flat!

Guess What?

Brit Debbie Wolf says she can make street lights fail when she walks past them. However, scientists are less convinced by her claims.

Stats 'n' Facts

Who: Zhang Deke
Famous for: Charging himself up with electricity.
Where: Altay City, China
Fact: With his electrical body, Zhang can also help people with ailments such as arthritis.

Testing Time

In 1994, Zhang was tested to see how his powers worked. Scientists said he had "a physical disfunction" but didn't explain what it was exactly.

Toilet Restaurant

The Modern Toilet Diner in Taiwan is exactly that ... a toilet-themed restaurant.

The seats in the diner are converted toilet bowls, and one of the most popular dishes is ice cream in the shape of a dog poo. Now, before you start thinking this is just a flash in the pan, you should know there are already more than 10 restaurants like this in Taipei City, Taiwan.

Squirty Man

Turkish construction worker Ilker Yimaz found out he had a special gift while he was swimming.

No, it wasn't that he could detect pee in the pool; he noticed he could squirt liquid out of his eye. The next step, of course, was to see how far he could squirt it. So, in 2004, he wowed the crowds by snorting milk up his nose and shooting it out of his eye in a stream reaching 2.8 m/9.1 ft. His milky antics gave him a world record.

Attack of the Giant Spiders

If you happened to be in Liverpool, UK, in 2008, you may well have nearly experienced a heart attack after being confronted by a 20-ton spider.

Constructed from wood and steel, the giant arachnid made its way down the streets of the city. The incredible machine was part of a street play production that saw the spider, named La Princesse, causing a spectacle over a five-day period.

"I wouldn't like to meet it in the dark."

Octogenarian Dorothy Wilson to reporters on how she first felt when she saw the colossal spider

Stats 'n' Facts

Event: Giant marching spider
Height: 15 m/49 ft
Cost: £250,000/ $325,000
Fact: Twelve people were strapped into the spider to control her creepy movements.

Squirt a Lot

It wasn't a good idea to stand too close to the scary spider. As she crawled along, La Princesse shot a huge spray of water from her abdomen!

Funny Foods

In the West, we like our food "normal" with a side order of fries. But to people from other continents, our tastes must seem very bland.

If you're driving down the road in Malawi, Africa, you may want to pull over and enjoy the local delicacy of a mouse on a stick. You can buy the dried-out mouse as a fast-food snack. Hungry readers will be pleased to know that the head, skin, and bones are all included in the price.

Mouse Rules

The correct way to eat a mouse on a stick is by beginning with the tail and working your way up to the head, spitting out the bones as you go!

Guess What?

In Southeast Asia, Cambodian spider is a delicacy. It's poisonous while alive, but when it's cooked, the critter's venom becomes harmless.

Prison Hotel

Ready to rest your weary head? Then hop on a plane to Germany, and visit the Alcatraz Hotel. This pit stop for tired tourists is a converted prison in the city of Kaiserslautern. You can spend the evening in one of the 57 "cells" available. A genuine prison bed is provided, along with traditional striped convict pyjamas. The windows are, of course, barred.

Nuts About His Bot

For those looking toward the future, you can do no better than to acquire a female android named Aiko.

Scientist Le Trung, who lives in Canada, has created a female robot that can remember faces, give directions, and understand over 13,000 sentences. Trung spends all his time and his savings on his fem-bot. He can be spotted taking her for a spin in the countryside or showing off her skills at technology shows.

Record-Breaker

Totally Crazy!

Most people would be happy to break just one world record in their lifetime, but not Ashrita Furman.

He has set 600 world records in at least 30 different countries in the last few decades. Here is a taster of his exploits:

★ Balancing a milk bottle on his head while walking for 130.2 km/80.7 miles

★ Crushing 53 eggs on his head in 30 seconds

★ Somersaulting for over 19 km/12 miles

★ Duct taping himself to a wall in 8 minutes and 7 seconds.

"If the stunt won't give you some joy, forget about it. A big part of setting a world record is to have a lot of fun!"

Ashrita Furman offers advice to wannabe world record-breakers

Guess What?

Ashrita Furman holds one extra-special world record ... he's the world record holder for holding ... well ... the most world records!

Scorpion Queen

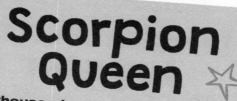

Five thousand scorpions, 33 days, and a 3 sq m/32 sq ft glass box ... Want to know more? Kanchana Ketkaew deserves her title of scorpion queen after she set a world record in January 2009 for spending the longest time ever confined with poisonous scorpions. The scorpion queen endured being stung by the pincer-wielding horrors 13 times during her record-breaking challenge.

Sting Me!

Kanchana is able to fight off the ill effects of scorpion poison because she has spent five years exposing herself to their stings in training.

Stats 'n' Facts

Who: Kanchana Ketkaew
Famous for: Sitting in a box full of poisonous scorpions
Where: Thailand
Fact: Kanchana was tearful at times during her record attempt, but she kept going.

Guess What?

Even though Kanchana's record attempt was difficult, she vowed to get back in her box if anyone tries to challenge it.

Underwater Juggler

In 2006, Ashrita Furman, the world's biggest record-breaker (see page 122), attempted to beat his own record for the longest time spent juggling underwater.

He set the previous record in New Zealand in 2002, with a time of 48 minutes and 36 seconds. For his second attempt in Malaysia, all was going well until 37 minutes and 45 seconds in, when a large shark bumped into him, causing him to drop one of his balls!

Fatal Fish

The Japanese enjoy eating fish, especially if they are poisonous!

The Fugu globefish is a delicacy in Japan, even though a deadly toxin can be found throughout its body, including its organs, membranes, and even its skin. To be able to eat the fish and actually survive, the skill of a specialist chef is required. It costs up to 20,000 yen (about £150/$200) to enjoy the thrill.

Bee-Movie Star

Playing the clarinet covered in bees is just one of Norman Gary's amazing tricks.

He's also appeared with bees on more than 70 television shows and six commercials, and he set a world record when he held 109 bees in his closed mouth for 10 seconds while they enjoyed a syrup-soaked cake.

"Whenever I make a mistake, I get stung. The stings can be prevented if you're very careful."
Norman Gary, the bee man

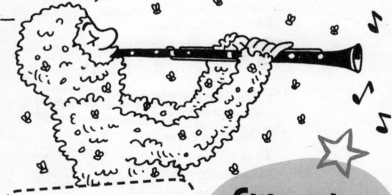

Stats 'n' Facts

Who: Norman Gary
Famous for: Getting up close and personal with thousands of bees
Fact: Norman looked after the swarm of bees that featured in the first X-Files movie.

Guess What?

Norman has worked with bees in films such as the Oscar-nominated Fried Green Tomatoes and ... um ... Invasion of the Bee Girls in 1973.

Hissing and Kissing

Totally Crazy!

Snake charmer Khum Chaibuddee must be crazy. This can be the only explanation for his attempt to break the world record for kissing the most poisonous snakes.

The event occurred in October 2006 in front of a Thai audience. They held their collective breaths as king cobras were individually released and then slithered their way onto the stage to be confronted by Khum with his puckered-up lips. Nineteen snakes later, and the job was finished, thankfully without incident.

Snake Smooch

Khum broke the previous world record for snake smooching, set in 1999 by American Gordon Cates, who managed to kiss 11 venomous snakes.

Guess What?

The king cobra is not the most poisonous snake, but it still has so much venom that it can kill an elephant, never mind a human being.

Stats 'n' Facts

Who: Khum Chaibuddee
Famous for: Kissing poisonous snakes, one after another
Where: Thailand
Fact: Medics were kept on permanent standby for Khum's snake-kissing record attempt.

Snail Bait

One minute, you're just a nine-year-old schoolgirl, the next you're setting a gruesome world record.

Tiana Walton is the world record holder for having the most snails sliming their way all over her face ... 25 of them, in fact. The rules for setting the record were strict but simple: Tiana had to put as many snails on her face as she could in one minute. Any snails that fell off after a 10-second period were disallowed.

"I am not squeamish. It is relaxing, but it feels a bit cold. They are quite smelly, and you can see their big long eyes."

Tiana Walton, snail lover

Snail Snout

Tiana's 25 snails beat the previous record of 15 snails. Her mother, Tommy, must be proud. After all, she set the world record for growing the largest lemon!

Stats 'n' Facts

Who: Tiana Walton
Famous for: Letting slimy snails crawl all over her face
Number of snails: 25
Fact: After Tiana's world-record attempt, the snails were treated to a gourmet meal.

Guess What?

Tiana's snail days are now behind her. She really wants to be an Olympic gymnast. Let's hope she can move faster than her slimy chums.

Hospital Food

Visitors to the DS Music Restaurant in Taiwan are in for a shock. You'd never guess from its name that it has a medical theme.

At the restaurant, you are served by waitresses dressed in nurses' outfits and receive drinks from IV drips mounted in the ceiling. If that's not enough, the decor includes wheelchairs and crutches, and if you need the bathroom, just look for the signs to the Emergency Room (Casualty).

Performing Pests

Many people think that they are fantasies, but flea circuses, where tiny insects perform incredible feats, actually do exist.

The Floh-Circus, held every year in Munich, Germany, is home to a show where fleas are put through their paces across several disciplines. These include flea soccer and flea-powered chariot races. The dog fleas used weigh less than an ounce and can pull objects that are an astonishing 20,000 times heavier than themselves.